Maasai

RENNAY CRAATS

www.av2books.com

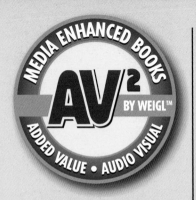

AV² provides enriched content that supplements and complements this book. Weigl's AV² books strive to create inspired learning and engage young minds in a total learning experience.

Your AV² Media Enhanced books come alive with...

Audio
Listen to sections of the book read aloud.

Key Words
Study vocabulary, and complete a matching word activity.

Video
Watch informative video clips.

Quizzes
Test your knowledge.

Embedded Weblinks
Gain additional information for research.

Slide Show
View images and captions, and prepare a presentation.

Try This!
Complete activities and hands-on experiments.

... and much, much more!

Go to **www.av2books.com,** and enter this book's unique code.

BOOK CODE

S 1 4 4 2 3 7

AV² by Weigl brings you media enhanced books that support active learning.

Published by AV² by Weigl
350 5th Avenue, 59th Floor
New York, NY 10118 USA
Website: www.av2books.com   www.weigl.com

Library of Congress Cataloging-in-Publication Data

Craats, Rennay.
 Maasai / Rennay Craats.
   p. cm. -- (World cultures)
 Includes index.
 ISBN 978-1-61913-171-2 (hard cover : alk. paper) -- ISBN 978-1-61913-531-4 (soft cover : alk. paper)
 1. Maasai (African people)--Juvenile literature. I. Title. II. Series: World cultures (AV2 by Weigl)
 DT433.545.M33C7 2012
 305.896'5--dc23

                              2011051106

Printed in the United States of America in North Mankato, Minnesota
1 2 3 4 5 6 7 8 9 0 16 15 14 13 12

062012
WEP170512

Senior Editor Heather Kissock
Design Terry Paulhus

Consultant Serena M. Tome
Chief Executive Officer, The Maasai Heritage Preservation Foundation, Inc.

Photo Credits
Weigl acknowledges Getty Images, Alamy, and Corbis as primary photo suppliers for this title.

CONTENTS

Where in the World?

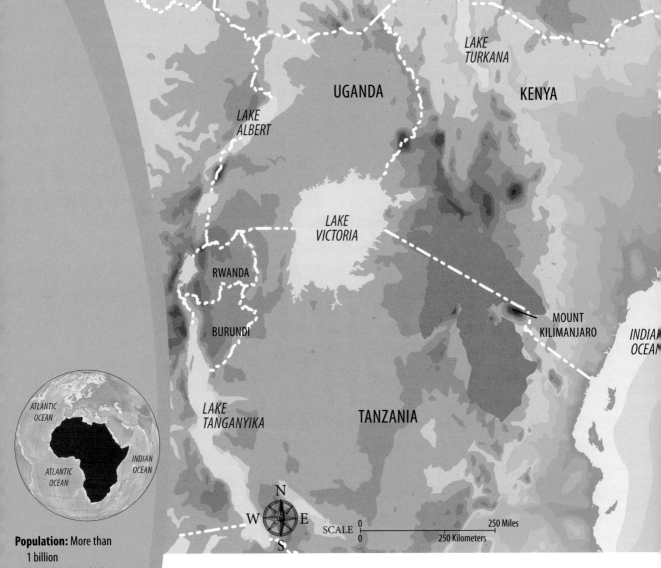

LAKE
TURKANA

UGANDA

KENYA

LAKE
ALBERT

LAKE
VICTORIA

RWANDA

MOUNT
KILIMANJARO

INDIAN
OCEAN

BURUNDI

ATLANTIC
OCEAN

INDIAN
OCEAN

LAKE
TANGANYIKA

TANZANIA

ATLANTIC
OCEAN

N

W   E

S

SCALE

0

0

250 Miles

250 Kilometers

Population: More than
1 billion
**Indigenous Population
(Maasai):**
About 883,000 worldwide
Continent: Africa
Countries: Kenya
and Tanzania
Area of Africa: 11.7 million
square miles (30.2 million
square kilometers)

The Maasai are **indigenous peoples** from eastern Africa. They live on the Serengeti Plain along the Great Rift Valley, not far from the border between southern Kenya and northern Tanzania. The grasslands in these regions are a good location for the Maasai to raise cattle. The Maasai are semi-nomadic. This means they move from place to place in search of the resources they need to survive. The Maasai travel to locations where there is grazing land and water resources for their cattle.

Maasai live in an area of about 61,770 square miles (160,000 square kilometers) in southern Kenya and northern Tanzania. It is uncertain how many Maasai live in these communities. Many Maasai do not participate in **census** polls because it is considered **taboo**.

Some researchers believe that the Maasai once lived in the Nile Valley in Sudan. They moved to the areas now known as Kenya and Tanzania around AD 1500. Researchers believe the Maasai brought their cattle with them when they moved.

It is estimated that the Maasai population is about 883,000 worldwide.

The word *Maasai* means "speaker of the language Maa." The Maasai are not the only **culture** to speak this language. There are two different groups of Maa-speakers in Africa. One group settled in communities and practices agriculture. The other group is nomadic. The Maasai belong to the nomadic group.

The Maasai have lived in Kenya since the 1400s. In the 1800s and 1900s, Europeans began exploring Maasailand. Over time, this European influence changed how the Maasai lived. While the Tanzanian Maasai continue to live more traditionally, the Kenyan Maasai live closer to large cities. Even the Maasai communities that have become more technologically advanced still value their traditions and beliefs.

Culture Cues

The Great Rift Valley is more than 3,000 miles (4,830 km) long. It stretches from Syria in Asia to Mozambique in southeastern Africa. This valley ranges in elevation from 1,340 feet (408 meters) below sea level to about 6,000 feet (1,829 m) above sea level.

It is common to see the name of these indigenous peoples spelled "Masai;" however, Maasai is the correct spelling.

The Maasai live in an area rich with history. For example, scientists have found human **fossil** remains in the area where the Maasai live. These fossils date back millions of years.

Mount Kilimanjaro is located in northeastern Tanzania near the Kenyan border. It is found in the eastern section of the Maasai's land. Mount Kilimanjaro is the highest mountain in Africa. It stands 29,035 feet (8,850 m) high.

Stories and Legends

Stories and legends help to pass on the traditions and knowledge the Maasai need to successfully live and raise cattle in the challenging environment of the east African plains.

The Maasai tell many stories about cattle. Other stories explain daily events in life, including death. Some stories explain the origins of the Maasai people and the gods they worship. For example, the Maasai worship a god named Engai. The Maasai believe Engai created everything on Earth and controls both life and death.

Engai comes to the Maasai in two ways. Engai can come to the Maasai in the rain and thunder that nourishes the grass for cattle. At this time, he is known as the Black God who represents good. Engai can also come to the Maasai as the angry Red God who is represented by lightning. Lightning strikes cause fires that destroy the cattle's grazing land.

The Maasai tell stories of Engai and his three children. One story explains how Engai gave each of his children a gift. He gave the first child an arrow, which the child used to hunt. He gave the second child a **hoe**, which was used to grow crops. He gave the third child a stick, which was used to herd cattle. The third child was a son named Natero Kop. He is considered the father of the Maasai people.

Cattle are the center of Maasai life and culture. Maasai culture was almost destroyed in the 1880s when 80 percent of their cattle were killed by a disease called rinderpest.

Cattle are an important part of Maasai stories and **legends**. The Maasai believe that in the beginning, the sky and Earth were one object. Then, Engai sent cattle to Earth on a rope.

The Maasai use the word *Ndorobo* to describe neighboring peoples. This word means "poor folk," or people without cattle. The Ndorobo peoples were hunter-gatherers. According to some stories, these people did not have cattle because they cut the rope. In other stories, the Ndorobo were startled at the sight and sound of cattle and cried out. This caused Engai to stop sending cattle. The Maasai, then, were trusted with all the cattle in the world. For this reason, the Maasai believe they are Engai's chosen people. This story explains why the Maasai are known to raid cattle from other tribes. They believe the animals must have been taken from them in the past.

A type of giraffe in Tanzania and southern Kenya is known as the Maasai giraffe. It lives in the same regions as the Maasai.

THE STORY OF
The Maasai's Arrival in Kenya

Originally, there were 12 tribes of Israel. These tribes took control of Canaan, the Promised Land, after the death of the biblical leader Moses. Eleven of the tribes formed the Kingdom of Israel. One of the tribes formed the Kingdom of Judah. The tribes scattered after King Solomon of Israel's reign ended. Only two tribes, Judah and Benjamin, remained. Over time, the tribes making up the Kingdom of Israel disappeared. Many believed the 10 lost tribes would be found one day. Some of the Nubians also traveled out of Egypt. Nubians are people from Nubia, an ancient kingdom in the Nile River valley. They intermarried and had children. The Maasai believe they are one of the "lost tribes of Israel." They began life in Israel before traveling to Egypt. From Egypt, they moved to Sudan and Somalia before settling in Kenya and Tanzania, where they live today.

The Maasai peoples' ancestors came from North Africa. They began traveling along the Nile River until they reached the areas between Lake Victoria and the Indian Ocean, and Kenya, Nairobi, and Tanzania in the 1500s. They lived in this region until British settlers arrived in the late 1800s.

Maasai warriors were well known to their neighbors. Other tribes feared them. These tribes put up little fight when the Maasai raided their cattle. As they traveled, the Maasai also took control over more land for their cattle.

In the 1840s, German **missionaries** became the first Europeans to encounter the Maasai. Two missionaries told stories of fierce warriors who were rarely challenged to fight. These fearful stories prevented Europeans from further exploring the area until the 1880s. During this time, a member of the British Royal Geographic Society became the first European to cross Maasailand. His name was Joseph Thomson.

Soon after, many other explorers traveled throughout the area. This brought hardship to the Maasai. Europeans brought **smallpox**

Timeline of the Maasai

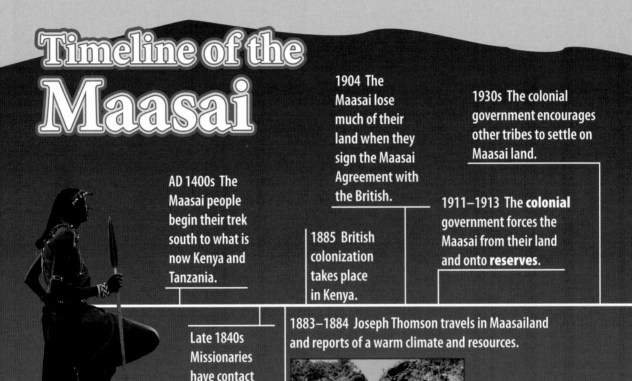

AD 1400s The Maasai people begin their trek south to what is now Kenya and Tanzania.

Late 1840s Missionaries have contact with the Maasai.

1885 British colonization takes place in Kenya.

1883–1884 Joseph Thomson travels in Maasailand and reports of a warm climate and resources.

1904 The Maasai lose much of their land when they sign the Maasai Agreement with the British.

1911–1913 The **colonial** government forces the Maasai from their land and onto **reserves**.

1930s The colonial government encourages other tribes to settle on Maasai land.

and other diseases to the Maasai. These diseases, as well as **drought** and cattle diseases, caused many problems for the Maasai. The entire culture was nearly destroyed. Other tribes took advantage of the Maasai's weakened state. These tribes stole cattle and territory from the Maasai.

In the early 20th century, the British government took control of two-thirds of the Maasai's most fertile land. During this time, the British government signed treaties with the Maasai. The government did not obey many of these treaties, and it took land from the Maasai. The government also created a railway, which crossed Maasai grazing land. The Maasai tried to fight against the British armies, but they did not have the resources to battle against British soldiers. The Maasai also tried to battle in court, but they did not receive a fair trial. The British administration passed laws that gave the Maasai reserves. The Maasai were not allowed to travel outside these territories. Others could not enter these territories. This prevented the Maasai from learning about new technology. However, they were no longer being influenced by European ways of life.

1991 Ethnic fighting occurs between groups in Kenya.

1974 The Maasai Mara National Reserve opens.

1963 Kenya gains independence.

1995 The Kenyan government renames the Maasailand "Makueni division" as it tries to take control from the Maasai.

1963–1978 Kenya's government continues to redistribute Maasailand.

1990–present The Maasai continue the struggle to reclaim their land.

1936–1946 The colonial administration introduces a cattle quota and reduces the Maasai's livestock numbers by about 70 percent.

1979 The new government is more considerate of the Maasai peoples.

2000 Maasai elders demand greater controls on trophy hunting by the government of Tanzania.

Social Structures

The Maasai are **spiritual** people. They believe that their god, Engai, gives each man a spirit. This spirit keeps the man safe. After a man dies, the spirit helps him travel to his resting place. Evil men travel to a desert. Good men travel to lush pastures filled with cattle.

The Maasai believe cattle were a gift to their people from Engai. Cattle are an important part of many Maasai **rituals** and ceremonies. A type of wild fig tree, called *oreti*, is also used in rituals. This fig tree appears in many legends as well. This strong, sturdy fig tree is a symbol of life.

Maasai culture relies on the leadership of the *Laibon*. Laibons are respected members of the Maasai community. The Maasai believe these

Women have a strong voice in Maasai society. They are responsible for purchasing beads and creating all of the beadwork the Maasai wear.

spiritual leaders, healers, and **prophets** are the children of their god. They are seen as a link between the Maasai community and their god. Laibons perform ceremonies and sacrifices. They also heal physical and mental illnesses. These positions are passed down from generation to generation.

The Laibon is very familiar with the plants growing in his surroundings. He knows which leaves, bark, or roots to use to treat specific ailments. The Maasai seek the aid of the Laibon to cure colds, infertility, malaria, and simple cuts. The Maasai continue to seek the help of these healers today. The Laibons treat conditions that cannot be treated with modern medicine.

According to Maasai **mythology**, the forest people taught the Laibons how to use plants as medicines. The Maasai believed the forest people are the ancestors of the Ndorobo and other hunter-gatherers.

Elders are highly respected in Maasai society.

THE SEASONS

The Maasai experience two different seasons. Each season lasts 6 months. The rainy season is called *alari*. It lasts from November until April. The dry season is known as *alamei*. This season lasts from May until October. The Maasai territory is coldest in July and August. The Maasai live and **migrate** according to these seasons.

Communication

The name Maasai comes from the word used to describe the Maasai language. The Maasai speak the language Maa. More than one million people in Kenya, Samburu, Camus, and Tanzania speak this language. People living on each section of Maasailand speak a different **dialect** of the language.

The spoken word is very important to the Maasai. Traditionally, the Maasai did not have a written language. History and legends were passed from generation to generation through stories. These

The Maasai sing to mark ceremonial occasions and while traveling. Warriors, girls, women, and elders have their own songs.

PLACE NAMES

The Maasai have borrowed words from other languages, including English, Arabic, and Swahili. Maasai words are used by other cultures, too. Many place names in Tanzania and Kenya come from the Maasai. The name for Kenya's capital city, Nairobi, comes from the Maasai phrase "that which is cold." Amboseli is a game park reserve in southern Kenya. Its name comes from the Maasai phrase "salty dust." The town Narok along the Great Rift Valley is named after the Maasai word stories explained the origins of the Maasai peoples and what happened to their spirits after they died. These stories were always told at night. The Maasai were busy working during the day and did not have much time to tell stories. The Maasai sing often. Herdsmen may sing if their cattle are well.

The tone with which the Maasai speak their words is very important. This helps listeners understand what is being said. The way the Maasai say a word can change its meaning. The Maasai make some language sounds as they inhale air. Others are said as air is exhaled. Some words require the Maasai to roll the letter "r" to create a **trill**. The Maasai use letters that are different from those found in the English alphabet.

The Maasai language has changed over the years. For example, the Maasai needed to name new events and experiences. Few Maasai have traveled outside of their territory. However, through tourism they have been exposed to different cultures. This has led to marriage among cultural groups. As a result, the Maasai created new words and ideas.

Like many other world cultures, the Maasai have created new meanings for existing words. As well, some words that are no longer used have been forgotten over time.

The Maasai record time in 14-year sections. Each section is named after an important person.

Other words have been borrowed from different languages, including English. For example, the word "book" has a similar pronunciation in the Maa language. It is said "em-búku." The Maasai lent many of their words and phrases to other languages as well.

meaning "the water that is black." This illustrates how early mapmakers encountered the Maasai and used the words to name places in these areas.

Law and Order

Similar to many other cultures, Maasai communities have rules that must be followed. These rules govern daily chores as well as marriage and status. The Laibon is a powerful man in the community. While the Laibon is actually a spiritual leader, this elder can influence group decisions as well. In the Maasai community, the elders make decisions as a group. The elders oversee religious ceremonies to ensure they are performed properly. They also settle disputes and decide punishments when rules are broken.

Each person in Maasai society has a specific role. Women gather firewood and cook meals.

Elders hold court, or council, to discuss specific issues. They determine how to resolve an issue and, in the case of rule breakers, they decide fair payment to victims. The elders address issues such as theft, inheritance, assault, and, on very rare occasions, murder. Fines for all **infractions** are paid with livestock. There are no jails. In some cases, people are physically punished.

Ownership and care of cattle are important issues in Maasai society. Maasai cattle are branded with a special mark. Each family group has a unique branding mark. This allows other members of the community to identify who owns the cattle. This prevents disputes about which family owns each animal.

Maasai elders oversee religious ceremonies. They also settle disputes when rules are broken.

The Maasai live in villages called *manyatta*. There are usually eight to 15 huts in a village. The Maasai build a thornbush fence around their villages as a form of protection. The thorns of the thornbush may be as sharp as barbed wire.

A Maasai village is built to protect cattle as well as people. The Maasai create a territory called a *kraal*. The men in the community build a fence around this space to keep others out and to keep cattle from escaping. The cattle are kept in the middle of the kraal to keep them safe from cattle raids. Cattle raids happen when other groups try to steal cattle from a Maasai community. Within the kraal, women build houses from grass and branches. They use cow **manure** to seal the outside of the houses.

Each Maasai person has a specific role in society. Women and children milk the cows and collect water. They also gather firewood and cook meals. The warriors keep the community safe from other tribes. The boys care for the cattle. The elders oversee the people, property, and daily events that take place in the village.

While young boys herd smaller animals, they learn to herd cattle as they grow older. Young girls build huts, look after younger children, and milk goats.

Celebrating Culture

In Maasai culture, each life stage is celebrated as a rite of passage. Men's lives are often divided into sections called age sets. People experiencing the same ceremonies and rites of passage are forever linked to that time. They belong to the same age set. Women do not belong to age sets. Instead, they are recognized by their husband's age set.

Special ceremonies and rituals mark each age set. Both male and female Maasai are **initiated** as they pass through several life stages.

Initiation begins when a Maasai baby is born. This event is celebrated. The women of the village eat ram meat. Then, they sing songs and bless the new child and the house where the child lives. As Maasai children grow, they receive many initiations. After each initiation, they are given more responsibilities around the village.

The most important initiation is called the *Emuratare*. This ceremony takes place when a boy or girl reaches puberty. After the ceremony, the entire village celebrates with a feast. The boys then become young warriors. The girls are married. Men marry when they are between 26 and 35 years of age.

During the *Eunoto* ceremony, a Maasai mother shaves her son's head. At this stage, the boy is considered an adult and old enough to marry.

Maasai men can have many wives. Having many wives is a sign of wealth. Before a man can marry, he must pay his bride's father with cattle. Each wife lives in her own hut. A man can marry as many women as he can afford to support.

Maasai boys look forward to becoming warriors. Warriors travel and live with other warriors. These men do not herd cattle. They protect the community and raid other tribes for cattle. After 10 years of living as a warrior, men become senior warriors.

The last age set is celebrated with the *Orngesherr*, or junior elder initiation. After a few months of preparation, a warrior's wife shaves her husband's long hair. After this, these men are no longer warriors. They become junior elders and are allowed to build their own homesteads. This is the final initiation for the Maasai.

Elders oversee everything in the village. They decide who will marry their daughters. They also ensure everyone behaves as they should in the village.

The Maasai are known for their jumping dance. Young men leap into the air from a standing position to show their strength and agility. Some men can jump up to 4 feet (1.2 m) in the air.

Maasai dress in bright clothing and jewelry for a marriage ceremony.

Art and Culture

Ornaments and jewelry are important parts of Maasai art and culture. These items are also used in ceremonies and celebrations. The women make jewelry. Men make their own spears, shields, and other objects that warriors use to hunt.

The Maasai are well known for their beadwork. They use about 40 different styles of beading. Some Maasai women apply **elaborate** beadwork to animal skins and clothing. They also create detailed necklaces, which both men and women wear. Necklaces can be narrow or as wide as the wearer's shoulders. Maasai women carefully choose the colors they use to create beadwork. Red is an important color in the Maasai culture. Red is often used as one of the main colors for necklaces. Then, smaller strings of different colors are added to the larger, red piece. Each bead color represents something that is important to the Maasai. Red represents blood. Blue is a symbol of their god. Green beads are used to recognize the gift of grass for their cattle.

In traditional Maasai beadwork, some colors cannot be placed next to each other. The Maasai believe ornaments that have these colors touching are ugly.

Maasai warriors do not hunt lions that are suffering from drought or have been snared or poisoned. It is forbidden to hunt a female lion unless she is a danger to humans or livestock.

The Maasai are great warriors. They prove their bravery through lion hunts. Maasai warriors hunt lions in groups of 20 to 40. They only hunt at certain times in order to allow the lion population to grow. They only hunt male lions.

At a hunt, the fastest runners lead the group. Those with the strongest shields follow behind. When a warrior sees a lion, he yells out to the group. The group then chases the lion into an open field. Warriors never sneak up on a lion. They believe the animal should have a fair chance to defend itself against its hunters. Some lions will run from the hunters. Others will fight. The Maasai surround the lion while one warrior throws a spear at the animal. Often, the lion attacks the warrior who threw the first spear. The other warriors block the lion's path and continue the attack. The first person to spear the lion is given its mane, paws, and tail. These are symbols of bravery. A successful lion hunt is a great achievement for warriors. The entire community celebrates this accomplishment. They do not celebrate if any warriors are injured during the hunt.

BODY ART

The Maasai often use their bodies as their canvas for artistic displays. Warriors use red **ocher** to decorate their bodies. They grind ocher into a powder and mix it with animal fat or water. Then, warriors cover their legs with the colorful mixture. While the mixture is wet, they make patterns and shapes on their legs with their fingers. When the ocher mixture dries, the pattern remains intact on their bodies. Maasai warriors use the mixture to dye their hair red, too. Women also use ocher to add color to their skin.

Dressing Up

One of the few clothing items the Maasai wear is a cloth, which they wrap around the waist and legs, and then throw over one shoulder. Maasai men and women also wear short skirts made from hide or cloth. Colorful robes called *lubegas* are a common clothing item in Maasai communities. These vibrant red or orange robes are unique to the Maasai culture. Some of these robes have patterns or designs. Others are made with bold, solid colors.

Maasai boys wear plain robes or **togas**. After being initiated, the boys begin to make themselves a headdress. They hunt many different birds for feathers to use on this headdress. They need the feathers from as many as 40 birds to make one headdress. A boy wears this headdress at dances and ceremonies. After the boys become junior warriors, they wear beaded necklaces.

In the past, the Maasai made beads from materials such as clay, shells, ivory, wood, seeds, and horns. Europeans brought colorful glass beads to East Africa. Today, the Maasai prefer to use these bright glass beads with smooth surfaces.

During ceremonies, young men wear a headdress made of bird feathers. Women wear beaded necklaces, headbands, and other adornments.

Boys wear beaded ornaments on their neck, arms, wrists, ankles, and earlobes. As warriors, boys can grow their hair long rather than shaving their head. Many warriors have long hair that they wear in small braids. They dye their hair using red ocher.

Young girls wear *shukas*. Shukas are wool blanket-like wraps. Once they are married, Maasai women wear wraps made from long pieces of cloth. Women often dye cloth or animal skins with ocher. They also add beaded patterns for decoration. Maasai women shave their hair. Many women wear brass ornaments that coil around their shaved heads. They also wear beaded necklaces and other **adornments**.

Only Maasai warriors are allowed to wear their hair long.

MAASAI JEWELRY

Maasai of all ages wear jewelry. Even babies are dressed in beaded necklaces, belts, and bracelets. Some babies wear **amulets**, which the Maasai believe will protect them from evil.

Both Maasai men and women pierce their ears. This process begins when they are about 7 or 8 years of age. When the right ear heals, the process is repeated on the left ear. One or two years later, a large hole is pierced in each of the child's earlobes. The hole is filled with a piece of a branch. Over time, the Maasai make the hole larger by adding wadded leaves. They wear beads and other ornaments in the holes. The earlobe hole may eventually be wide enough to fit a fist through. The Maasai believe large earlobes are a sign of beauty.

Young boys and girls are not allowed to wear fancy jewelry in their upper ears. They can add beaded strings or decorated leather pieces. As they get older and enter new age sets, they can wear more detailed jewelry. Necklaces and headdresses can be very elaborate. Only married women can wear long blue beaded necklaces and beaded flaps on their earlobes.

Food and Fun

Cattle are important to the Maasai's diet. Cow's milk nourishes adults and children. It is also used to make yogurt and a substance similar to butter. Cows are very valuable. Therefore, the Maasai do not often kill them. They are killed for their meat on special occasions, such as the birth of a child or an important ceremony. By killing a controlled number of cows, the cattle population remains stable.

The Maasai are respectful of cows. They practice certain rituals after killing these animals. The Maasai will not eat a cow's meat and consume its milk on the same day. They believe that doing this will make them sick. Maasai will choose to either eat meat or drink milk in a day. The Maasai also believe it is disrespectful to drink the milk of a living cow and then eat its meat after it has been killed.

Herding cows is a great responsibility for Maasai boys. They must protect the herd while making sure the animals have enough food and water.

Maasai Diet

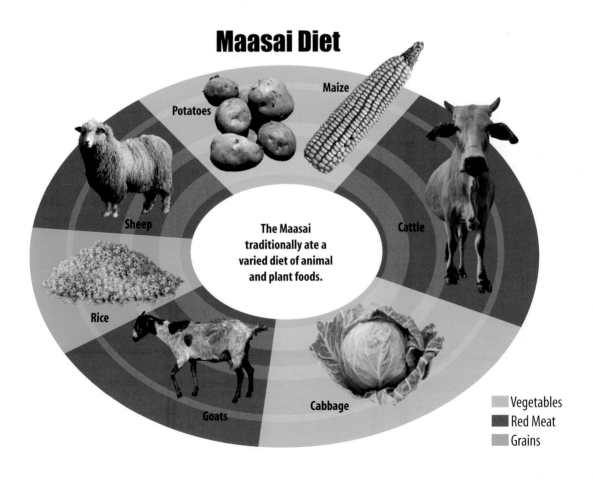

Potatoes

Maize

Sheep

Cattle

The Maasai traditionally ate a varied diet of animal and plant foods.

Rice

Goats

Cabbage

- Vegetables
- Red Meat
- Grains

The Maasai share their food with the entire community. Everyone who has not consumed milk will eat when an animal is killed. They use every part of the animal to make everything from containers to clothing. Cow's blood was traditionally an important part of the Maasai's diet. They believed that drinking the blood of a healthy cow would make the tribe strong. The blood was also nutritious. Blood provided the people with much needed iron and protein. The Maasai often mixed the blood with milk. They would then drink the mixture. The Maasai usually drink this blood and milk mixture during the dry season.

Today, the Maasai's diet consists of many food items. The Maasai herd sheep and goats in addition to cows. They eat these animals during feasts and ceremonies. Their diet also includes maize, rice, potatoes, and cabbage. The Maasai trade for these products. Few of the Maasai farm. They believe farming ruins the grazing land.

Foods play an important role in many ceremonies. For example, during the milk drinking ceremony, elders give warriors milk to drink. This occasion marks the moment when a warrior is able to drink milk alone. Prior to this ceremony, a warrior must not drink milk without the presence of another warrior. Following the ceremony, the warrior's family slaughters a sheep to eat during the celebration.

The meat-eating ceremony takes place at the end of a warrior's career. At this time, a man can eat meat in the presence of an adult woman. This occasion is celebrated with a feast of oxen and honey beer.

Ceremonies often determine which foods the Maasai should eat and when they should eat these foods.

Ugali Recipe

- With an adult's help, bring a pot of water to a boil. Add salt and butter to the water.
- Once the water is boiling, stir in flour until the mixture thickens. Remove the pot from the heat, and let it stand for 5 minutes.
- Return the mixture to low heat until it becomes a large lump. Then, remove the pot from the heat, and let it stand for another 5 minutes.

Great Ideas

The Maasai do not farm. They also do not eat beef often. Traditionally, the Maasai obtained the nutrients they needed without harming their sacred cattle. This practice is called bloodletting. Bloodletting provides the Maasai with iron, protein, and calories without slaughtering the animal. The process is also useful when there is not enough milk for all members of the community to drink. The Maasai mix blood and milk together so there is more liquid to nourish more people.

During bloodletting, the Maasai drain some blood from a cow. The animal is not harmed. To obtain the blood, the Maasai first tie a strap around the cow or bull's neck. Then, they wrap an arrow with a strip of leather. The arrow is dulled so it does not enter too deep into the animal's neck.

Bloodletting must be done carefully so that the cow is not injured or does not lose too much blood. The blood is mixed with milk. This mixture is a staple of the Maasai diet. Today, some of the Maasai are replacing this mixture with cornmeal and milk.

A warrior carefully pierces the cow's **jugular vein** with the dulled arrow tip. The blood is collected in a container called a *calabash*. Once the Maasai have collected the blood from the animal, they remove the strap from the animal's neck. The wound is packed with a bit of manure or dirt to help stop the bleeding. The animal is also lovingly stroked to keep it calm. When the bleeding stops, the animal is released. It does not suffer any permanent injuries.

Bloodletting is practiced throughout the year. It is also done on special occasions, such as a child's first initiation ceremony. All ceremonies include the ritual of drinking blood or a mixture of blood and milk. When women give birth, they are also given blood. This helps them regain their strength.

The Maasai collect cow blood in calabashes. Some are highly decorated.

Warrior Weapons

Maasai warriors use many different weapons during battles and ceremonies. The Maasai are very skilled with these weapons. They use shields to defend against attacks. Some warriors use swords that are sharp on both edges. Others prefer a rounded club that is used to beat the enemy. Sometimes, they throw this club at the enemy, too. The spear is the most important weapon for warriors. Maasai spears are made in three sections. The long shaftlike center is made of wood. Both ends of the spear are made from steel. One side of the steel spearhead is sharpened to a point. The other side is left dull. The steel ends are attached to the wooden grip using hardened wax. The Maasai hurl the sharp end of the spear at enemies or animals. Next to cattle, the spear is the Maasai's most valuable possession.

At Issue

Land is important to the Maasai—both for their cattle and their culture. In the past, young boys built and lived in their own village as part of their initiation into manhood. This tradition is dying because there is not enough land.

The Maasai have struggled with land issues since the early 1900s, when British settlers began exploring their land. The British realized the value of the land and the natural resources. The British government took control of a large amount of land that the Maasai used for grazing.

This trend continued, even after Kenya and Tanzania became independent from Great Britain. The new governments focused on using the land for agriculture rather than raising cattle. These governments also used the land as a way to attract income from tourists.

Tourists from all over the world come to Kenya and Tanzania to see wildlife in its natural state. Millions of tourist dollars flow into local economies each year. Parks and reserves have been created to protect wildlife and the environment and to promote tourism. When creating these parks, governments sometimes have shown little concern for indigenous peoples. Parks have been created without considering the needs or rights of the Maasai.

Some of the Maasai have privatized their land. Many herders joined together to own land and create group ranches. However, this has kept the Maasai and their herds from moving to new locations for grazing as the seasons change.

The Maasai have attempted to change policies by **lobbying** the government. Their efforts have been largely unsuccessful. Six of Tanzania and Kenya's national parks were created by forcing the Maasai from about 5,000 square miles (13,000 sq. km) of land.

Government officials claim that the Maasai overgraze the land and that their cattle compete with wildlife. In fact, the Maasai keep only the number of cattle necessary to sustain their way of life. They also take special care to ensure the land can adequately support their cattle. The Maasai have lived alongside wildlife for thousands of years without harming the environment or the animal populations.

The Maasai have organized to lobby for their land and way of life. This is not easy for the Maasai since they lack funds. The Maasai have also launched education campaigns to let people around the world know the problems they face.

International organizations have come to the aid of the Maasai. For example, in the Ngorongoro Conservation Area, the Maasai have been given animal health training, Maasai women have become cattle owners, and water management projects have been built.

The Ngorongoro **Pastoralist** Survivalist Trust was formed to address the Maasai's rights and the management of the Ngorongoro Conservation Area. It is working to convince governments to include the Maasai in important decisions and allow the Maasai more control over their land.

The Maasai Environmental Resource Coalition

The Maasai Environmental Resource Coalition (MERC) is a group of Maasai people who are working together to preserve their traditional lands and the rights of their people. The coalition hopes to save east African ecosystems from habitat destruction, as well as protect the Maasai's traditional ways of life from being forgotten in favor of modern technology.

Since the 19th century, disease and the forced removal of the Maasai from their land have harmed the culture. Governments continue to force the Maasai from their land in order to promote economic development, tourism, farming, and habitat destruction. MERC raises awareness of these issues in an effort to reclaim Maasailand and respect for the culture.

Through education programs, MERC is helping Maasai communities become more aware of the issues they face. MERC also works with local and national governments to ensure Maasai rights are recognized.

Into the Future

Until the 1960s, the Maasai did not practice private ownership. At this time, the British government began a program to buy and sell Maasailand and livestock. Before this program was implemented, the Maasai could not sell livestock for money. This new development forced the Maasai into world markets. Plots of land were made into ranches that were managed by individuals or groups. This development has caused problems within the Maasai community. Some Maasai, as well as other Africans and foreigners, became very wealthy. Others became quite poor.

Some plot sizes are too small for Maasai to raise cattle. The Maasai are forced to survive by farming. This is insulting to many Maasai people. They believe that farming is not a natural activity and that it ruins the land for grazing cattle.

In recent years, the Maasai have adapted to the new ways of the world. Many people in the community are receiving formal education. They are also part of a new **eco-tourism** industry.

The Maasai live peacefully with wildlife. They share their land with these animals in parks and group ranches. This helps the Maasai receive income from tourists. Money paid by visitors to these ranches helps maintain the Maasai way of life. The money is also used to send Maasai children and adults to school.

Technology is causing many Maasai people to stop practicing their traditional ways of life. The Maasai have lived the same way for hundreds of years. Now, they must change their culture in order to survive. As the Maasai lose their land, they can no longer raise cattle. This could result in the end of their culture. Many Maasai are trying to prevent the loss of their land. They are working hard to preserve their culture and traditions for future generations.

The Maasai have had to change their culture to survive. Many Maasai children now attend school.

Role-play Debate

When people debate a topic, two sides take a different viewpoint about one idea. Each side presents logical arguments to support its views. In a role-play debate, participants act out the roles of the key people or groups involved with the different viewpoints. Role-playing can build communication skills and help people understand how others may think and feel. Usually, each person or team is given a set amount of time to present its case. The participants take turns stating their arguments until the time set aside for the debate is up.

THE ISSUE

The Maasai way of life has changed significantly in recent decades. The government and private individuals have taken much of the traditional Maasai land to use for farming and wildlife conservation. Some Maasai have been forced into individual ranches, restricting their ability to move livestock with the seasons. All of these factors have forced many Maasai to reduce the size of their herds. Some have been forced into poverty, and their traditional culture is in danger of being destroyed.

THE QUESTION

Should the governments of Kenya and Tanzania encourage agricultural development on traditional Maasai lands?

THE SIDES

Maasai: Agricultural development prevents the Maasai from grazing their cattle, especially in areas that have access to water.

Government: Planting on more land will help feed our people and help our economy grow.

Ready, Set, Go

Form two teams to debate the issue, and decide whether your team will play the role of the Maasai or the role of the government. Each team should use this book and other research to develop solid arguments for its side and to understand how the issue affects each group. At the end of the role-play debate, discuss how you feel after hearing both points of view.

World Cultures Quiz!

1 In which countries do most of the Maasai live?

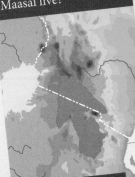

2 What does the word *Maasai* mean?

3 What is the name of the god worshipped by the Maasai?

4 Who was the explorer Joseph Thomson?

5 In Maasai culture, who or what is a Laibon?

6 What does the word *Ndorobo* mean?

7 The rainy season called *alari* occurs during which months?

8 Who settles disputes and decides punishments in the Maasai community?

9 What is the Maasai word for village?

10 How does a Maasai warrior prove his bravery?

ANSWER KEY

1. Kenya and Tanzania 2. speaker of the language Maa 3. Engai 4. He was the first European to cross Maasailand. 5. a spiritual leader, healer, and prophet in the community 6. poor folk or people without cattle 7. November until April 8. the elders 9. manyatta 10. through a lion hunt

Key Words

adornments ornaments that decorate the body

amulets items worn as charms against evil

census an official count of the population

colonial a country that conquers and controls a distant country

culture the customs, values, beliefs, and traditions that people share

dialect the words and pronunciation used in a particular area

drought period of extreme dry weather

eco-tourism educational travel focused on conservation of the environment

elaborate detailed or complicated

fossil the remains or impressions of a person or an animal that lived millions of years ago and has hardened in rock

hoe a tool with a flat blade and a long handle that is used for farming

indigenous peoples the first settlers in a country or region

infractions breaking of rules or laws

initiated admitted into a society or group, often with special ceremonies

jugular vein a large vein in the neck that carries blood to the head

legends traditional stories of earlier times

lobbying a campaign to try to influence government policy

manure animal waste used to fertilize soil

migrate leave one place and settle in another for part of the year

missionaries people who travel to spread the Christian faith

mythology ancient stories that explain cultural traditions

ocher a red or brownish mineral made from clay and iron oxide that is used to create color

pastoralist cattle or sheep farmer

prophets people who can predict the future

reserves areas of land that are set aside for a particular purpose

rituals activities that are part of a ceremony

smallpox a contagious disease caused by a virus

spiritual having to do with the spirit; not of the physical world

taboo something that is banned

togas loose flowing outer garments

trill a vibrating sound

Index

Log on to www.av2books.com

AV² by Weigl brings you media enhanced books that support active learning. Go to www.av2books.com, and enter the special code found on page 2 of this book. You will gain access to enriched and enhanced content that supplements and complements this book. Content includes video, audio, weblinks, quizzes, a slide show, and activities.

Audio
Listen to sections of the book read aloud.

Video
Watch informative video clips.

Embedded Weblinks
Gain additional information for research.

Try This!
Complete activities and hands-on experiments.

WHAT'S ONLINE?

Try This!	**Embedded Weblinks**	**Video**	**EXTRA FEATURES**
Map the area in which the Maasai live.	Learn more about the Maasai.	Watch a video of the Maasai dancing.	**Audio** Listen to sections of the book read aloud.
Write a biography about a well-known person from the Maasai.	Read about the history of the Maasai.	See how the Maasai live today.	**Key Words** Study vocabulary, and complete a matching word activity.
Create a timeline showing the history of the Maasai.	View the arts and crafts of the Maasai.		
Draw a chart to show the foods the Maasai eat.			**Slide Show** View images and captions, and prepare a presentation.
Test your knowledge of the Maasai.			**Quizzes** Test your knowledge.

AV² was built to bridge the gap between print and digital. We encourage you to tell us what you like and what you want to see in the future.
Sign up to be an AV² Ambassador at www.av2books.com/ambassador.